Main

BOA
EDITIONS LTD

the
black
maria

the
black
maria

poems by
ARACELIS GIRMAY

2015 WHITING AWARD WINNER FOR POETRY

AMERICAN POETS CONTINUUM SERIES, NO. 153

BOA EDITIONS, LTD. ✳ ROCHESTER, NY ✳ 2016

First Edition
16 17 18 19 7 6 5 4 3 2

For information about permission to reuse any material from this book please contact The
Permissions Company at www.permissionscompany.com or e-mail permdude@eclipse.
net.

Publications by BOA Editions, Ltd.—a not-for-profit corporation
under section 501 (c) (3) of the United States Internal Revenue
Code—are made possible with funds from a variety of sources,
including public funds from the Literature Program of the National
Endowment for the Arts; the New York State Council on the Arts, a
state agency; and the County of Monroe, NY. Private funding sources
include the Lannan Foundation for support of the Lannan Transla-
tions Selection Series; the Max and Marian Farash Charitable Foun-
dation; the Mary S. Mulligan Charitable Trust; the Rochester Area
Community Foundation; the Steeple-Jack Fund; the Ames-Amzalak Memorial Trust in
memory of Henry Ames, Semon Amzalak, and Dan Amzalak; and contributions from many
individuals nationwide. See Colophon on page 120 for special individual acknowledgments.

ART WORKS.
arts.gov

State of the Arts

NYSCA

Cover Design: Sandy Knight
Cover Art: *Sea* by Aracelis Girmay
Interior Design and Composition: Richard Foerster
Manufacturing: McNaughton & Gunn
BOA Logo: Mirko

Library of Congress Cataloging-in-Publication Data

Names: Girmay, Aracelis, author.
Title: The black maria : poems / by Aracelis Girmay.
Description: First edition. | Rochester, NY : BOA Editions Ltd., 2016. |
  Series: American poets continuum series ; 153
Identifiers: LCCN 2015043256| ISBN 9781942683025 (paperback : acid-free
  paper) | ISBN 9781942683032 (ebook)
Subjects: | BISAC: POETRY / American / African American. | POETRY / African.
  | SOCIAL SCIENCE / Black Studies (Global). | SOCIAL SCIENCE / Emigration &
  Immigration.
Classification: LCC PS3607.I47 A6 2016 | DDC 811/.6—dc23 LC record available at
http://lccn.loc.gov/2015043256

BOA Editions, Ltd.
250 North Goodman Street, Suite 306
Rochester, NY 14607
www.boaeditions.org
A. Poulin, Jr., Founder (1938–1996)

And there are stars, but none of you, to spare.
—June Jordan, "Sunflower Sonnet Number Two"

CONTENTS

elelegy

the black maria

❋

elelegy

———————

*It is estimated that over 20,000
people have died at sea making
the journey from North Africa to
Europe in the past two decades.
On October 3, 2013, it is
estimated that 300 people died
at sea off the coast of Lampedusa.
Those on board the boat that
sank were nearly all Eritrean.*

*This cycle of poems focuses on
Eritrean history, as this is a
history I am somewhat familiar
with as someone of its diaspora.
But, of course, the history of
people searching for political
asylum and opportunity (both)
is much larger than Eritrean
history alone.*

elelegy

who

I, *Aracelis Kay Weyni Girmay, the narrator-author, born in the United States. My routes: Eritrea, Puerto Rico, African America.*

we, *the living*

you, *unless stated otherwise, the dead*

the sea, *also a "you," talkless "witness," body of water, body of bodies*

the Luams, *there are four Luams. One Luam is nine years old, she is the sister of Abram, Alexander Pushkin's great-grandfather, who was kidnapped, sold into slavery, & given as "a gift" to Peter the Great in the early 1700s, it is said that Luam drowned or died at sea, here she is also a fish, or the dead; one Luam is 36 years old, she was born in Asmara, Eritrea but now lives in Umbertide, Italy, outside of Perugia, where it is idyllic & quiet, & she cleans houses there; one Luam is 36 years old & lives in New York City, where she teaches school & writes poems, & she was born in the United States; one Luam is 36 & lives in Asmara where she is a nurse at the hospital. Luam means "peaceful" & "restful" in Tigrinya.*

the flies, *the word "angel" has come to English from the Latin "angelus" & the Greek "angelos" which mean "messenger, envoy, one that announces." The Old English word for it was "aerendgast" which means "errand-spirit." For the Luams there are no angels, only flies.*

About the flies the Luams say: The fly is bright & working. It carries the messages of hunger & the sentences of the wound. It cannot carry the message without, itself, being touched. The fly whose hands & feet touch death, bring death to where it lands. Out of doors, it carries the history of the wound, disobeying the locks on doors & screens. The flies, they are the honest who know their history & take it everywhere.

Romare's Odysseus, after the legendary king of the Odyssey epic, Odysseus was famous for the ten years it took for him to return home after the Trojan War. Romare Bearden painted & collaged this Odysseus as a black man in the Black Odyssey cycle which concerned black travelers on their way to & from home.

when

1702, 1530, 2013, 1781, 2015…

"Still, all the history of the world
happens at once." —Jean Valentine, from "Then Abraham"

where

New York City, one of the largest natural harbors in the world. Before colonization, New York was an area of land inhabited by Algonquian-speaking tribes, it was since colonized by the Dutch, Portuguese, & British. Today, it is the most linguistically diverse city in the world, & the most populous city in the United States. Along with London & Tokyo, it is one of the three "command centers" of the world economy.

Umbertide, a small Italian town in Umbria, not far from Perugia.

Asmara/Asmera is the present-day capital of Eritrea. It was once part of a region called Maekele Bahr (named to describe the land between the Red Sea and the Mereb River). The area was later part of a medieval kingdom called the Medri Bahri, or Land-Sea/Sea Land. Evidence suggests that the city's origins trace back to 800–400 BC. Asmara was under Italian occupation from 1897–1941, & under British occupation from 1941–1952, after which Eritrea was "federated to" Ethiopia, making the new capital Addis Ababa. In 1959, Ethiopian authorities introduced an edict which established the compulsory teaching of Amharic (the language of Ethiopia's ruling class) in all Eritrean schools. In 1962, under Emperor Haile Selassie's rule, Eritrea was officially adopted as Ethiopia's 14th province. Between 1959–62, an Eritrean independence movement began to form which turned into a 30-year war for independence that was won in 1991. Theoretically the state is a unicameral parliamentary democracy, but the president & former freedom-fighter, Isaias

Afwerki, has been in office since independence. National elections have not been held since independence, over 20 years ago.

the Mediterranean Sea
the Red Sea
the Caribbean Sea
the Atlantic Ocean
the Afterworld Sea/Sea of Death
any Sea

The typewriter hammers out
the end of its ribbon,

as you, one by one,
go & go & go,

outlasted,

by memory,
by ink,

the patience
of the paper

where the dark words buck
like fish in air.

I, The Living.
Which is

my portrait?
The right hand

bleeding the page
for its marrowmarks

or the silence my left hand

inherits?

While the room is still
dry here,

while the page is still
white, still here,

more shore than sea, more still
than alive, while the air is now

touching the dark & funny fruit of
your eyebrows where it is quiet enough

for me to hear the small sighing
of your shoes lift up into

the old & broken boat,
while the small hands of water

wave, each one waving
its blue handkerchief, then

the gentle flutter of luck
& tears. We all know

what happens next. Do not go.
But if you must,

risking what you will, then,
in a language that is my first

but not your first, & with what I know
& do not know, I will try to build

a shore for you here, a landing place, here
where the paper dreams

that you will last. Our parents
& our grandparents taught

us: in the school of dreaming,
the discipline of dreaming.

It is my work: to revise & revise,
even as you are filling my eyes, now,

& you are filling the sea (Courages).
& the fishermen drop their veils

into your grave.

The sea delivers
your letters, the reams of paper,

the ink & messages
& shells telling us "goodbye."

Goodbye, you say,
to them, to that, goodbye,

to the city in which for lunch, for dinner,
we ate the moon, its theater of faces,

its sweater factory, the cathedral
bells ringing stoically above a fit of sparrows,

the cafés whose doorways seem to weep, now,
with the red & amber weeping of beaded curtains through which

the months blow in & out, invisibly
as months, as old men.

Goodbye your somewhere where
the President stands in uniform

wearing a peacock, pinned-alive,
to his chest. Through

his binoculars he sees this & that, approving, disapproving.
He does not understand the degrees of love.

The difference between your love for country
& your love for him. His memory has long skin, it counts

the invasions, the factories & ports & rails.
Each British motor. Each Italian nail.

Each machine that was built,
then dismantled by

the Allied Forces of the great
& "moral" war. His memory counts

each bullet, each fire,
each beautiful bone

of each person felled
in the street.

But the President
& his long memory, they think they know

better. They order the children. They cut the news
& power. They decorate the country with

paper offices & send the young
to forever-service where they carry guns

& patrol the streets & Badme
& the borders cut sloppily as beginner's cloth.

The distant ugly sharpen their knives
& look greedily on, in wait.

You, cousins, are the children of the ones who stayed.
No one has to tell you about commitment,

about love, you who grew beneath
the eucalyptus trees

& the grey faces of the martyrs
framed on the bedroom wall.

There are your aunts, your uncles.
The coffin-eye static of the photograph holds

your mother, your elder,
your one. You wanted

to live, to study & to make
things. To be free. In a war-land

the birds all sing
the saddest songs

of people who will not write poems
about their feathers or learn their calls & names,

so busy are they waiting for news of The Gone
& burying, without bones, their dead.

King Leopold II was the founder of
the Belgian Kongo. His regime was responsible
for 2 to 15 million Congolese deaths.

In the Kongo there are wooden statues:
bodies covered in spikes & nails. Each nail,

it is tradition, marks a wound
& promises retaliation. I think of King Leopold

& how he lived for ten decades,
& how his country & children lived.

& how the Kongo dies still fertile & green with the dead
& with trees & with army. These statues did not work

the way the maker imagined. The way
I would imagine.

Today, just over a hundred years later,
hundreds & hundreds of these bodies stand

in museums, in books,
on shelves, the dark, wooden bodies

swollen with the rusted & silver scales of nails.
Grief & wounds on display, the black docent

(is he me?) explains: The coins we pay
to view them will not ever go back to the dead,

& will not go to the living. In their cases,
they will gleam like fishes. On another continent,

on the radio, a man listens to a Tigrinya song
repeat & repeat something that means, more or less,

Eritreans, as fishes!? & yet again, it is you
on that ship, stuttering across the sea.

You have placed it on the scale
of the ocean, weighing life against life,

& again you lose, are shimmering
with the silver sorrow of

a thousand arrows,
a thousand nails.

It is October, 2013,
off the coast of Lampedusa,

the Italian fishermen whose
grandfathers, nearly a hundred years ago, barred

our grandfathers from
our grandfathers' land

& streets, in whose armies our grandfathers fought
against the beautiful bodies of their own neighbors, these

grandfathers meet again through you
& the fishermen who,

some of them, pull you from the sea, who,
some of them, watch you drown

out of ruin, out of hate, out of fear. *Jesus,*
Mary, who forgive us,

you are the ugliest trick.

What world is this,
my world, your world of wealthy thieves

holding the guns to your heads,
breaking your cervixes & bones

while the rest of us light our candles & buy lipsticks.
How is anything able to grow as we theorize about purity & rhetoric?

Italy, Israel, my United States
of blood-laws & carmine, always preserving,

always looking back into the faces of
"our fathers," policing the map

of a mouthless land. In my countries of genocide,
I implicate myself & dullen on

these sneakers & these meats,
until I have filled my home

with this & that, & to my deaths
amass amass amass.

Beloveds, beneath the surface
of your last place, the tiny, oblivious fishes

form wreaths above the sea grasses
& their long reach—

Some mornings, in my own city far away,
I run to greet "you" come to me as sea, & carry

myself out into your long, dark time like a child meeting
its older cousins. I touch your teeth & give you the single word of my body.

I am a woman again, at the side of Aboy Haile's bed. Aboy who is 96.
He is brushing my acacia hair. He is holding my arm.

He says, moving his hand to mean "all around us,"
that this is my home. He means Adi Sogdo,

but he also means the world.
Though I think, in "America,"

that I am There &
he is Here, that we are different, or far,

really, we are each other. *My bones are
your bones*, he says. His teeth are my teeth

& my smiling is his smiling.
He holds my arm tight, until it is a stone, a bone.

He smooths my hair
with force. I am a horse.

The long, dark skin of the water,
the talk, talking Aboy of the water,

the brushing back, brushing back my acacia hair,
washing my face. When we are done

I cross the sea back into air
& return to the traffic of the streets I know.

I am marked by the dead, your sea-letters
of salt & weeping.

Now I am ready to lay my self down
on the earth, to listen to the instructions

for how to talk of love & land, to sing
of home in the horrible years, & to fill

my language, like the stars do,
with the light, anyway, of a future tense.

to the sea (any)

I mark, obsessively,
the route,
the family-piercing
of the map
in place after place:

                .

    .   .   .   . .

                .   .

    .   .   ·········· ···   .

      .   .   .   ······· ·· ·····   .

                .   *(sea)*   .

        .

Adi Sogdo, Gondar,
Arecibo, Chicago, Nairobi
Griffin, Santa Ana:

        A series of holes
scar the paper with space
nearly flooded by you,
your blue dimension
who seams below
the flat surface of
our passages
above which, again,
we are the shipped.

.

& when it happens,
you, or me,
but always you, actually,
& more brutally,
into the sea's greater silence,

you
who slept in a different room
of a large house, but you
whose face I loved, whose face I knew

．

you are going now
into that other realm
without kerars, the goat's hide stretched
across the drum, you go
going now, with your perfect feet,
your one hand of red nails,
your folded sweaters & jackets,
hair, unaccompanied by horns
& the songs you know, you go
going far from where
you started, having been born,
having not ever arrived,
inside a wooden casket now
livid with the anonymous rose, inside
a catholic church beside the sea,
preyed over by the symbolic grief
of government, & no one allowed
who knows your name, to claim you,
though there is a table back home
& donkeys you knew, & your brother,
right now, is fixing his son's bicycle
in the land whose every changes
you had words for, & your brother
is telling his son now that you
are on your way, he is using
the present-tense to talk of you
though above their heads the kashmiri tree
is already stirring with Shiva & fruit

"Take this warm, white gabi to wrap yourself in."
—Reesom Haile, tr. C. Cantalupo

.

hands for pleasure, hands for mending
shirts, hand for making & for taking,
hands for killing, hands for cutting,
hands for eating, feeding, shutting,
hands for writing, hands for
touching the ears of donkeys,
hands for washing, hands
for cooking & for tea, hand for
brushing your sister's hair,
hands for injera, hands for prayer,
hands for building the "house-
hand" for feeding chickens,
hands for holding hands,
for kohl, for carrying books,
hands for guns, hands for sleeping,
but hands for doing nothing,

hands for touching his face,
hands for wiping tears,
but the handlessness of water,
the handlessnesses of sky & boats,

the sea, handless, having "evolved"
without them, unable to do
how the handed do,   yet, the distance
& the ushering of the dead

————into————

the distance.

after Patrick Rosal

to the sea (any)

Born without the order
of our roles, our seeing, our language,

you carry what is human
without being human.

All of it foreign to you
as our hurt is foreign.

Your lack of human speech
& body, whose body

we project our own onto.
Our losses, our desires.

       Sea-
blackness, our Eurydice,
at the shoreline when we ask,

Where are our dead, have you carried them
back to us? You repeat only,

Who, who?

       with a line after Rainer Maria Rilke's "Orpheus. Eurydice. Hermes."

"black, full of language"
                    —Celan

What I know about water: the sea,
the river, the faucet, the moon,
waking us in the night, voyeuristic
in the confusion of sleep, what is that
saying?

about what I know about
the beckoning of all that blue muscle,
a kind of beast pawing at the bluff(s),
it is always carrying some otherelse
almost here. We live with its taunts & improvisations so:
sea's a queen, ours, killing us & lullaby.
After "where" & "how much," "sea" was
the other word I knew, but now my ear is black
& fool of her language.

[I see Romare Bearden's "The Siren Song" & cannot help but think of you.]

Odysseus, his lungs full
of air, the sailors, their ears

full of wax, their lack
of will, then their will,

Odysseus' hearing,
the white froth

of gull, salt lapping at
the boat's brown skin,

the strange syntax of
his body's phrasing,

perpetual blue,
the perpetual blue

through which we read
his struggle, his

body is a black flag
wounding the pastoral

scene. I want to taunt
ship, to do two

things: call you Home
& deliver you Away,

revise the birth
of that hateful passage

by which you, Romare, & we.

[In one corner of the sky, near the horizon line, Romare Bearden has signed his name. The name "Romare" means "Rome."]

Claim, I, to be the poet, making talk
the sirens who foreground the scene

where even the sky sings *More air, More air.*
Romare, Romare, whose body is a mourning sound

(blood hyphened by the fleet
to Saint Domingue, to Rome), is

siren speech. But listen closely.
It is *my* mouth wailing redly

into the scene from The Future Knows.
It is my history raiding me. Romare,

teach me how to read this blues, please,
differently. How not to

assign all blackness near the sea
a captivity. I, the descendant

of each early war, who cannot remember peace,
have taken hostage the greenness

of my own mind. Want
the sirens to be

only the sirens. The sea
to be only the sea. O, magnolia

without blood, blackness
without blood.

.

_____

The febrile & opal
beauty of jellies,
pleasingly toothless, yet
        their passive, handless terrorizing, their

pearlescent softness there-thereing.
Systolic & slow, go
the long-legged
        hauling of the agonies

to the three worlds
of lightlessness & light,
bearing the common message
        of the commonness of fire.

to the sea near lampedusa

for the eyes we closed for
safety & distance   for

,

the freedom we wasted
on things

,

the terrors our acts lit
into the wet retina of
your memory   if you should

,

call it that

,

for the years you behaved
in a distance that was not
quite distance as we burned
our fires   each other & you

,

handless   please—the silence

,

is what we feed what burns
in the bright absence of The Living
they were   swollen in flower

,

shirts & in boots
meant for the earth
but not for you

luam to the dead
        —umbertide

The news announces
your last place:

a picture of rocks & sand.

Having slipped through the *seam*
of one realm into another, through
into The Lost where
hours no longer touch you,
we wait & wait.

A figure catches in the street!
Your color, your height.
The rareness of both in this town.

But you are the nothing now
except what history carries in its dog teeth.

Life, my luxury, my room alone
at the hill's green foot.
My view of racket & deer.

At night I run the shower to warm me.
The water, it comes
suddenly, cousin,
my hand
through you.

[It is said that Abram Petrovich Gannibal, the great-grandfather of the poet Alexander Pushkin, was born at the end of the 17th century in a village called "Lagon" in Eritrea. Historians assert that it was probably Logo TsaEda or Logo Chiwa. At the age of 7 he was kidnapped & sold into slavery in Constantinople. He eventually was ransomed to the Russian capital where he was given as a gift to Peter the Great. He is the subject of Pushkin's unfinished novel known in English as *Peter the Great's Negro*. In November 2009, a statue of Pushkin was inaugurated in Asmara, the capital of Eritrea, to commemorate Abram's legacy. Other sources state that he was originally from Cameroon. It is important to say here that the story of Abram is no more special than the stories of countless & anonymous others who were kidnapped & sold from all over the continent, as property, as gifts. Those girls & boys, those men & women, were, too, the parents, grandparents, children, sisters, cousins of poets & makers, some of whom have lived to tell the story, some of whom have not. *In their shapes, this poem is written.*

In some of the stories, Abram Petrovich Gannibal had a sister named something like "Lahan." I will call her, here, Luam, which is a common Tigrinya name. Tigrinya is just one of the languages of present-day Eritrea. In Tigrinya "Luam" means "peaceful" or "restful." The Luam/Abram stories vary. In some, she is said to have been taken captive alongside her brother but then to have died after being brutally raped (all rape is brutal) at sea. In one version of her story, she is said to have chased after the boat that took her brother. She leaps after him, & drowns. In another version, she is taken hostage on the boat but she dives into the sea & dies while attempting to escape, to swim away home. The story of Luam, in each of its versions, is the story of many, in Eritrea & outside of Eritrea, who have fled or attempted to flee, whether carried away by bandits, dreams, or, most common in the 21st century, by the consequences of a thoroughly devastating post-colonial legacy which often leaves its subjects with lack of other choices but to attempt to flee/leave into the diaspora.]

luam/ asa-luam
        —the afterworld sea

there was a water song that we sang
when we were going to fetch river from the river,
it was filled with water sounds
& pebbles. here, in the after-wind, with the other girls,
we trade words like special things.
one girl tells me "mai" was her sister's name,
the word for "flower." she has been saving

this one for a special trade. I understand
& am quiet awhile, respecting, then give
her my word "mai," for "water,"
& another girl tells me "mai" is "mother"
in her language, & another says it meant,
to her, "what belongs to me," then
"belonging," suddenly, is a strange word,
or a way of feeling, like "to be longing for,"
& you, brother, are the only one,
the only one I think of to finish that thought,
> *to be longing for*
> *mai brother, my brother*

luam, who says to the dead,
      —sea near lampedusa

I saw the hundred
fishes from a distance
& this is what I knew:

they were not fishes,
they were you.

Inside the sea, there is more
than sea:

---

rockets	shoes in pairs	luam
amphora	icarus	gold earrings
debris	the photographs	his once-wings

---

though it seems, from this distance,
a flat blue line—actually, a purling there:

the dead move mammalian through
its buried light,

& a graveyard is built
out of history & time

．

The black-eyed woman,
we will call her Azieb,
whose brother traveled with her
town to town, across the deserts,
& then into the other country, & the next,
where they said goodbye, as was
their plan, before, finally,
the month when she was taken
out to the boats, & below
her breath she began to sing
the wedding song that goes *Now
you will stay with your husband's
family*, she had no husband
but imagined distance to be
the one she married, the one
she walked with beneath
the wedding laurel, the one
her brothers lifted in the husband
chair, she sang, & those who were around her,
those who could hear, they touched their chests
& suppressed tears, not for their country
(for what was that?) but for their hills & zigni,
the melancholy of their parents' names,
Rahel, Zainab, Goitom, & the true laughing
of their sisters, their dark & leopard gums
flashing, their teeth,
the memory of cafés & Binyam
whose stories were always good.
There were the bare feet
of the black-eyed woman's words that,
even bodiless, wandered. She sensed
in her skin that the sea was an ear itself.
She did not know what to call this feeling,
so called it "Luam," & sang for it.

Having captured your beauty in a picture
He thought to keep you for himself

It was a wolf who tore your parts
But time caught him, & he is gone.
　　　　　—Asres Tessema, from *Letters to Asmara* (1991), tr. with G.K.

[The Obelisk of Axum was erected in the 4th century AD & was probably used to mark the site of an underground burial chamber. In 1937 it was shipped, as war booty, to Italy, where it was erected in Rome. It was not returned until 2005. Today there are 8 ancient Egyptian obelisks still standing in Rome.

rhyme (n.)- agreement in terminal sounds]

To be near sea is to gleam
　　　　　with dream, though to cross
means loss. But behold
　　　　　the gold & strolling
"nobodies" cajoling,
　　　　　& the frees off running
from lead & gunnings to
　　　　　the bleak audition.
& then: transmission
　　　　　over sea, they flee
& flee & flee from home
　　　　　toward Rome,
in pieces on ships
　　　　　like the obelisks.
Then reaching, not reaching.
　　　　　Then coffled into coffins.
The leadened news.
　　　　　The citizen dead. A crime
to live, a crime to leave. You left.
　　　　　All of us visiting the world.
Some counted as more,
　　　　　some counted as less.

with a line after Gwendolyn Brooks

42

luam in the sea, to the survivors
        —sea near lampedusa, the afterworld sea

Boat by boat, you inch the tightrope
thinly, together. Every now & then stopping
for your eyes to follow, into dark space, the brother
who would not last. The Galaxy does not blink for this sadness. Churns on.
Though you throw your faces down after, over
the relatives now little bones, & sand.

Remember to be what the berbere made you: lit
with red life, the holler of survivor's blood—
Remember your names from when we were green.
When History was little.

luam remembers massawa
—umbertide

There, small hills of salt
on either side of the grey road,
the blue sky & the sun burdened with sun.
White mounds & beige flats.

This is what is left
of an evaporated sea
separated from
the rest of the sea.

One is you, one is me.

Distance: my wealth.
Distance: my grief.

luam to her sibling
  —umbertide

Slowly, I shed the mind's black hive,
its small hairs & figures, its sense,

& slowly I lose & lose my salt,
& weep & leak, for I am warm, & breathing

among the piazzas & bakeries
& windmills while

the trafficked & drowned, one by one, lose
their breaths. The grief of chocolate

stores, the grief of dress shops in the year
of the sea. Last October,

you ran your errands in Asmara,
to & from the market, & now.

          Somewhere in our city, a little boy delivers tea
in small & sturdy glasses. The customers drop small coins

into his hand & pat him on his shoulder. The tea,
it is the color of someone's eyes,

yours or the hyena's staring out
of a cage. The woman who is selling fruit,

she fills my bag with oranges,
for today, for tomorrow, for the next day.

(So many oranges we fool ourselves
into thinking we will live forever.)

We are in Keren again. It is raining
in Asmara, I know, because it is July

& Adey used to call crying Binyam
July-August face.

As you go down
you are not remembering any of this,

not the fields, not the spoons of sugar
you counted over our mother's tea.

The kettle is whistling.
This is what it meant to be alive.

What can we do but sing of details, all of them minor,
in the year of salt & death—

luam cleaning house
—umbertide

Moths, moths,
this is our
shelter, what
one of our kind
made for another
of our kind.
That Last Light you saw
was not a moon
but an invention
to keep me safe
from stumbling
up the walk,
or to help me to see
what it is
at the door.

In the morning
your bodies, shavings
of flight, here & there,
having surrendered.

You were always dying
in my sleep.
& I, your last
neighbor.

Before I take the brown broom
gently to your body,
I see your once-was.
With care, I study your eyes.
It is my job.

the luams speak of god

If there is a god, let it be the hyena
who plunges her mouth into the river after eating
our grandfather's poisoned bait, who,
dark with thirst, poisons the river
unbeknownst to both of them.

Her ghosts stand in the street where we are called
already through "time" out of our houses. She tells
her stories. We tell her ours. We all clean our teeth
with what is sharp. She asks, *Will you add this*
story to your stories of history & land & peace?
Yes, we will add this story. We ask her,
Will you add these poems to your repertoire of songs
about hunger & thirst & fur? & she, being wiser than we,
says, *Yes, I will sing them if*
you grant me your permission
to turn them into poems about
a mercy.

luam
        —new york

The flies, six
in a metallic pile, identical
green, identical
bristle & gaud.

To see so clearly
the science
in their suits.

And yesterday, the woman
asking, Are you twins?

My sister & I, whose
mothers are different,
whose years are.

From a distance,
are we, species by species,
identical? Each other.
Our needs & moving. Dear Fly,

my Other Life out
splintering, involved
in the evolution:

we are like siblings,
you & I, separated
by many years, & rooms.

luam

    —asmara

See how they wear black & blue
to the funeral, how they crawl
& how they fly, touching what is dead
with the smallness of their hands
& feet, a beautiful theory
of arches in their wings.
How they carry
pieces of the uncle
to the stones

& sprinkle our bread
with the city's milk, & skin.

No one loves the flies, their work,
their rearranging, marking us
with the light of other guests.

Religious world—

if there are angels, they are flies
who hover over our privacies,
kissing us with mouths
that have kissed
other wounds.

luam & the flies
      —umbertide, asmara, new york, october, 2013

It was the end of the world.
The world was ending. I sat

in my house with the flies. Though
the night was dense, was long, we

tried to wait for light, to last.
But the wind at the doors. &

darkness knuckled, flashed its teeth.
Outside, the other houses,

outside, the solitary
field, tall singularity

of the mama tree. What was
strong was razed, what was alone.

I thought we would, plural, survive.
But I saw the deaths of flies.

I watched them clean their wings &
faces, then die in the night,

watching quietly out &,
looking, facing it. Morning

I saw them at the windows
as though remembering the

green, last world. Their legs curled in
the syllable of struggle,

or sleep. I counted six awes
who died in the night, whose sounds

died in degrees. Trying to learn,
I picked them gently up by

their wings & studied, then placed
the six onto one, white plate:

six corpses or comas, six
I tried to see but took to

the window & poured them out
for the dirt & rosemary.

       If I were moored to place, if
I had believed that this would

always be my home, if I
were to be lucky. One day

their descendants would be mine,
would handle my death, too, with

their small legs, yellow mouths &
wound-hungers. Powerless to

brush them from my teeth & eyes,
I'd be bright finally with

their taking, a city of
eggs, a harvest, an "&"; oh,

emerald signage of bodies.
I would be a kind of port

or harbor—Finally, them
again.

Look! In other poems you are.

Making & delivering the tea,
fixing the bicycle, reading the map,
answering the phone! Turning
the bulb of light into its socket.
I cannot decide. Are the poems
brilliant for not letting you go?
Or misinformed? Or stupid?
Or worse?

Daily I am looking for signs
of what has lived & what is lost.
From a 5th-story window
a plastic bag is falling, lightly now,
slowly down. I make a god & deal
with it. I say, If I catch it in my arms
then you will live!

The wind takes hold. The street.
The neighbor's yard. The street,
the street. Which is more cruel?
Believing or not believing?
I sit down in the road & rock
the bag's loose & fallen shape
while the muscle contracts
—it is a serious game I play—
like a camera, I shutter—open,
close. Among the dead:
       You. Not you.
       You. Not you.

The dead are always
       You. Not you.

luam mending clothes
  —umbertide

The life of my thread,
as I pull it through the clothes I mend,
is long.

The life of the cypress rows
& the roof of the house
in a time of peace
in a country that bled
ours dry for its peace
is also so long.

But the life of my flies
at the windows, in the yard,
covering the fruit,
bringing messages, always,
of the dead, their lives
are not long. Every second
they acquaint me & acquaint me with
the littleness of their deaths,
the ticking we are, each, built with.

It is true. For now, I live
& must love everyone.

Second I Borrow,
Breath I Borrow,
with you I will mend
the clothes of strangers.

luam

 —*new york*

Back when I was small,
smaller than I know is true,
a tiny man collected my coins,
arranging them in
the rectangular darkness
of the payphone like silver
moons by which he wrote
his quiet codes of news & births
& whispered them into
the cackling & chameleon wire.
I thought that if
I starved him of the moons I dropped,
neat wreaths of light
by which he seemed to write
The Severances, that we
would, simply, live,
that he held, in fact, a kind of key,
like the angel Azrael who,
I read, transcribes & erases all
the names of the living, the births & deaths,
&, they say, is covered in eyes
& tongues, a set for every person who is alive
thus constantly changing shape
for accuracy. If I could short-circuit
the wire, somehow fumble the data,
I'd trick it all, or throw a wrench
in the wheel: no loss, no death.
But I know now
Azrael is small, & god is
small, smaller than
we ever supposed, tiny,
actually, & captive. Governed by
what governs us,
but more or less alone, transcribing inside the dark law

of our story & will,
dutifully following
the orders. How could we
expect them to understand exactly what goes on?
The dark cost of our laughters & our weeping.
The hours spent
on our knees trying
to trip the wire & pacify
the divinities
instead of walking out of doors
& out of rooms. Small mimicries,
small scribes, small nons we nourished,
on whom we wasted
all of our light & verbs.

luam
  —monterchi, italy

I am told that we are here
to ask the Madonna for help, to bless
our wombs & husband-salt & children,
to consider the future, the beauty of
a world crowned by pomegranates in damask
& identical angels wearing socks.

La Madonna is beautiful, but in repose
there is more her face reveals,
the knowledge of angers, or death.
She is dressed in the lazuli dress,
one could say, of the mountains, the blue dress
of history, the always splitting
world on the brink of splitting,
her dress touched only by
the hands of men who clothed her, piece by piece,
the miners shoving their hands
into the mountains of Badakhshan,
then the men of Venice & later
to the hands of Piero, in Monterchi. Hands, so many that
when the baby comes no one will know
to whom the child belongs. It will be mixed
with earth & sea & distance.
For this birth,

let us credit the girl, or name the wars or
a sensuousness, Piero or the mountains,
but not god, not the angels.

to the sea

great storage house, history
on which we rode, we touched
the brief pulse of your fluttering
pages, spelled with salt & life,
your rage, your indifference,
your gentleness washing our feet,
all of you going on
whether or not we live,
to you we bring our carnations,
yellow & pink, how they float
like bright sentences atop
your memory's dark hair

.

Why not, in addition, tell
the story of laughter,
your father's heart a found-bird
mending, tucked inside
the body inside the parked car
where an auntie warns
he should not laugh so hard
because he is still healing
and *It's not so good. For your heart.*
Once, Abrehet could not stop laughing,
just like you are now. So
she had to go to the hospital.
No one had seen anything
like it before.
The story is a drizzle
turning into rain.
She laughed for five days straight!
No break! Even for food!
She couldn't breathe!
She almost died!
They had to look for medicine!
Maybe they would have kept her
forever! Not a lot of people know
that laughing can be dangerous
for you if you don't watch out!
Which makes us laugh harder, even now.

It is common for cries to be mistaken
for gulls, for whistling to sound
like the wind.

I am listening in
on the last century,
with my ear to the door.

But there is no mistaking laughter.
It is laughter.

.

strange earth, strange
that we will die into

this bright, blue oblivion
though the day is beautiful

& later, the night will
also be   (beautiful)

with the noise of crickets who,
even as we lose & lose make

their bodies creak
with desire & the dusk,

& we will call these sounds
"the future continuous," us

to the sea

You who cannot hear or cannot know
the terrible intricacies of our species, our minds,
the extent to which we have done
what we have done, & yet the depth to which
we have loved
what we have
loved—

the hillside
at dawn, dark eyes
outlined with the dark
sentences of kohl,
the fūl we shared
beneath the lime tree at the general's house
after visiting Goitom in prison for trying to leave
the country (the first time),
the apricot color of camels racing
on the floor of the world
as the fires blazed in celebration of Independence.

How dare I move into the dark space of your body
carrying my dreams, without an invitation, my dreams
wandering in ellipses, pet goats or chickens
devouring your yard & shirts.

Sea, my oblivious afterworld,
grant us entry, please, when we knock,
but do not keep us there, deliver
our flowers & himbasha bread.
Though we can't imagine, now, what
our dead might need,
& above all can't imagine it is over
& that they are, in fact, askless, are
needless, in fact, still hold somewhere
the smell of coffee smoking

in the house, please,
the memory of joy
fluttering like a curtain in an open window
somewhere inside the brain's secret luster
where a woman, hands red with henna,
beats the carpet clean with the stick of a broom
& the children, in the distance, choose stones
for the competition of stones, & the summer
wears a crown of beles in her green hair & the tigadelti's
white teeth & the beautiful bones of Massawa,
the gaping eyes & mouths of its arches
worn clean by the sea, your breath & your salt.
                    Please, you,
being water too,
find a way into the air & then
the river & the spring
so that your waters can wash the elders
with the medicine of the trying of
their children, cold & clean.

to the sea

our dead whose words you cannot know
& so you are protected from the dense contagion
of that sadness, so take them then (our messages & theirs)

what would it cost you?
nothing

praise the water, now,
praise the last room,
praise the carrying to
& the carrying away,
its salt stitch & always going on
with its back to dominion, & country,
praise the water who helps us to see
our smallness by
not seeing us, who
helps us face oblivion, oblivion
& live, & know that we'll choose
flowers still
& the pure, black trying
of the crickets.

I love the azucenas, so bring them to you,
& beles in August from Alem's hands,
Alem who is the best seller.

I love the rain when it is hot & raining.
& the color of beets, the color of shiro
in the kitchen jar, the sound of bees,

the word "werKi" & the word "shukor"
& the slow, high flight of the soccer ball
& the water-sound of my love's guitar.

There is also your face that I love.
Your face, a red & gorgeous word
in a long sentence of a long story.

& I love the large silence of the baobab tree,
the quiet of the desert quiet,
the red & laughing mouths of

the bougainvillea. I love
the pepper & the hay,
the nervous hunger of

the fat squirrel with his hand
on his heart, so bring them to you.
& I bring, to you, my father, or yours,

someone you loved, anyway, who was older,
saying, over the water, *Ambessa, Ambessa,*
as if you could hear him, as if it were you.

the luams

[In ancient Egyptian mythology, Isis, sister-wife of Osiris, goes out looking for her beloved's body, which has been scattered, in pieces, all over the earth by his jealous brother. I am thinking of this story as a version of the story of Luam & Abram (as Isis & Osiris), but also as a story of dismemberment, migration, diaspora. For this reason, the voice of the poem is plural—to accommodate the voice(s) of the different Luams in this cycle. The kite in stanza two refers to the bird known for its scavenging for parts (food) & its associations with funerals & Isis.]

First, our footsteps
             this way, that,
up the mountain, then down.
             In the river, then out.

Then my wings, my
             sister-body a red kite's.

We find you scattered
             there & here & there,

your body a fluttering
             procession of ants
carrying fruit,

in the sea, your body
             in the boat of hours, your
body in the road on
             the news, there & here & there,

we find you, then, & with
             our thread & letters sew
you back, neatly, piece by piece,

hawi, our broken book
             (at night we dream
as we assemble you

we, too, assemble our rage,
                its hands & mouth, though
we must choose, in the end, which:

the poem of healing
                        or
the poem of poisons).

The sun is shining now
                against our forehead.
We will stay this shape if it means
                you will live, not
as you did before, but in the trees,
                the silt of the river, unkillable as
the hush of air traveling through
                Adey Zuphan's corn

on poetry & history
    —after Joy Harjo

On a panel of men who spoke about history & poetry, she sat quietly for much of it. They, the men, were saying strong things, good things but in authoritative voices, voices that knew they knew things. & she remained the only quiet one. She listened as if she weren't listening. Her face looked forward. Her quiet seemed distant. It had a straight back. & then she interrupted one of the men & said something like, "That reminds me of the time…" & she spoke of a fellow Native American teacher in her region who committed suicide near the end of one of the years, & how he must have been hurting & isolated & in pain, but not many people spoke about that, or spoke about his death or their loss when he died. It was swept under the rug, that was the phrase she used, & she said she was at home one day & looking out of the window & she noticed a black thread or string there, floating in the frame, & she observed it for a while, floating there, until she realized that that black string was grief. The grief of the professor, the grief of the students, her own grief, the grief of silence, a historical grief, & that she knew that it was her job to take that thread & put it somewhere, weave it into the larger tapestry (she made a gesture, then, as if that tapestry were just above her head). She said it was her job to put that grief in its place, or else someone else, some child or grown person would be out walking & just walk right into it, without knowing what it was they'd walked into, what they had, then, inherited in a way, what they were, then, carrying & feeling. The danger of that. The grief of that. & that was what she said about poetry & history. & that is all I remember from all of the things that were said that entire day.

the black maria

george jonathan almaz malcolm shewit renisha kimani trayvon angel jason vincent biniam
abraham lolita suheir solmaz joaquin angelita huey assata marcos etheridge lucy francisco
phillis june cisco bob patrice spotted elk roberto jayne lucille sekou yohannes girma henok
khadija aster dennis andrew audre gloria toni henry carmen khaled idris maya addie mae
cynthia carol denise paula gunn bessie mercy to others awet flor

[maria, plural of mare: any of several mostly flat dark areas
of considerable extent on the surface of the moon or mars…
though *mare* means "sea" in latin, they lack water.
–merriam webster • astronomers thought the lunar features
were seas when they first saw them through telescopes.
these dark basins were referred to as "black maria." basins
and craters misidentified as seas.]

I don't know if you have known anybody from that far back, if you have loved anybody that long, first as an infant, then as a child, then as a man. You gain a strange perspective on time and human pain and effort.

Other people cannot see what I see whenever I look into your father's face, for behind your father's face as it is today are all those other faces which were his. Let him laugh and I see a cellar your father does not remember and a house he does not remember and I hear in his present laughter his laughter as a child. Let him curse and I remember his falling down the cellar steps and howling and I remember with pain his tears which my hand or your grandmother's hand so easily wiped away, but no one's hand can wipe away those tears he sheds invisibly today which one hears in his laughter and in his speech and in his songs.

I know what the world has done to my brother and how narrowly he has survived it and [. . .] this is the crime of which I accuse my country and my countrymen and for which neither I nor time nor history will ever forgive them, that they have destroyed and are destroying hundreds of thousands of lives and do not know it and do not want to know it.

—James Baldwin, from "A Letter to My Nephew"

THE BLACK MARIA

black the raven, black the dapples on the moon & horses, black sleep of
    night & the night's idea,
black the piano, white its teeth but black its gums & mind with which
    we serenade the black maria.

    & the night, wearing its special silver, serenades us, too,
    with metaphors for how the body makes: semen stars, egg moon.

1600s: European ships heave fatly with the weight of black grief, black
    flesh, black people, across the sea; the
astronomers think the moon's dark marks are also seas & call them "the
    black maria."

    Meanwhile, the Italian Riccioli, naming the seas according to his
    language & sensibilities.
    Riccioli naming the dark fur of the moon:

Mare Cognitum, Mare Crisium, Mare Fecunditatis; Sea that Has
    Become Known, Sea of Crises, Sea of Fertility.
If it is up to Riccioli, then these are the names of three of the black maria.

    I call the sea "mar." I call the sea "bahri."
    I call the moon "luna." But "far" is my word for both you & the moon.

I heard a story once of a woman in the Sahara who, for years, carried a
    single page of *Anna Karenina*
that she read over & over, the long combers of print repeating like the
    waves of the black maria.

    Language is something like this. A hard studying of cells under a
    microscope,
    cells on their way to becoming other things: a person, a book,
    a moon.

Above the bowl, I crack the egg of this idea. Yolk from clear. Which is It?
Which is Not It?
Does "moon" name the whole thing, or just the side we know, the side
made dark with the black maria?

How language is an asha tree, a fool that grows everywhere, a
snake shedding its skin.
A bowl of teeth. A kitchen plate of shadow & ruins, like the moon.

Moon says, "Please, god, crowd my loneliness with stars." But the star's
life is short compared to Moon's.
There is always a funeral. Moon is always wearing the veil of the black
maria.

However pretty the sound, it was a misidentification,
to name the basalt basins & craters the black maria of the moon.

If this is a poem about misseeing—Renisha McBride, Trayvon Martin,
Rekia Boyd,
then these are also three of the names of the black maria.

Naming, however kind, is always an act of estrangement. (To put
into language that which can't be
put.) & someone who does not love you cannot name you right, &
even "moon" can't carry the moon.

If this is a poem about estrangement & waters made dark with millions
of names & bodies—the Atlantic
Ocean, the Mediterranean & Caribbean Seas, the Mississippi, then these
are also the names of the black maria.

For days, the beautiful child Emmett swells into Tallahatchie. Even
now, the moon paints its face
with Emmett's in petition. Open casket of the night, somebody's
child, our much more than the moon.

THIRD ESTRANGEMENT, IN MEMORY OF JONATHAN FERRELL

This morning I left my house
to talk about love with my girl,
but already, her head in the news,
so I began the walk back. Through the fog,
to my right, over my shoulder,
I heard the hunter whistling to his dogs.
He was near. In the fog's white heart,
I worried for my legs, their arms,
all of us dark & bare, without oranges
or flags. I will be mistaken, I thought, for another
animal, one it is legal to kill. A bear or boar.
& none of my noises distinctly human.
Bear me. Bore me. My animal breaths
& words. At the end of the road,
someone's mother is playing at
the accordion again. A stack of cars,
junked, on the back of a truck.
Her third hand waves to me
in the old Italian way of waving,
which looks like "goodbye" but also like "come."
Of the eight directions, I cannot tell which
is safest. Only that, somehow, I would go on & on
if up to me. Then the ground on which to lay
my body down, following its flatness.
When their hands are upon,
I know I am mere story, a hornless curiosity
bleeding out to space the space of me
that was secret even to me.
I say my words, but they, to
them, are *nothingspeaking,*
so stand, so stagger, stagger
to present the humanness of my plea,
but I am bucking in moonlight, to the emptying clip.
Of my dance away from the gunning they would say

the same manies: Urgency. Athleticism. Grace:
the muscles, vexed, in strain & falling.
I turn my face & try to rid my head of knowledges.
Instead long for the shape of the cypress,
but a consequence is thinning me.

I am a farness now, & the moon's black maria.

THE WOODLICE, FOURTH ESTRANGEMENT

The beauty of one sister
who loved them so
she smuggled the woodlice
into her pockets & then into
the house, after a day's work
of digging in the yard,
& after the older ones of us
had fed her & washed,
she carried them into
the bed with her, to mother
them, so that they would have
two blankets & be warm, for
this is what she knew of love,
& the beloveds emerged one
by one from their defenses, unfolding
themselves across the bed's white sheet
like they did over 400 years ago, carried
from that other moonlight,
accidentally, or by children, into
the ship's dark hold, slowly
adapting to the new rooms
of cloths, then fields, & we,
the elders to that sister, we,
having seen strangers
in our house before, we, being
older, being more ugly & afraid,
we began, then, to teach her the lessons
of dirt & fear.

THE FIG EATERS, FIFTH ESTRANGEMENT

& there was the beauty of one sister
who was wild once, though you
will not believe or see, at first,
how she drew dark in the sun
& grew the blackest hairs
in the back of her house
where she climbed the trees
barefoot, the ten tiny toenails gleaming
like newborn, would-be claws,
& her shyness before us, the older two,
made her silent yet she climbed
& climbed, swiftly, roundly, happily,
as a way of speaking & showing what
she knew to do & loved, into
the tree's green & yellow head
to pluck the slow jewels of the fig eaters
from their habitat, those bugs whose mouths
were made only to eat what is soft
already, what is worn with rot, & whose mouths,
for we were not among the hunters,
had not evolved to hurt us, & the sister,
catching them with her hands, coaxing
them to ride her arms & hair before
toward us they rose out of the talon,
which did not know it was a talon,
in the new garden of our father's house
which was not the first garden, but the second,
paradise without dangers, as it should be, at least
in the beginning, where, in the narrow kitchen,
behind the strangely groomed bushes
cut into the shapes of spheres & animals,
never sat a bowl of figs I would have washed
for him if this had also been my wilderness
for they, the figs, were never saved,
& really, really we knew already that all the garden

could grow was the small girl & the world of beetles.
The heavy heart-sacs of the figs looted outside of the house,
whose purple cerebra heaved
with a familiar strain of starlight (ours), whose
plural green deaths fed the beetles &,
thusly, the sister, too, who,
in the absence of "real" siblings,
inherited the father & the yard, not greedily,
but truly, which made me stop
thinking, then, of our father's grief
in our absence from his country & his custody & house.
The plates & cups now used again.
The closets now filled with small & empty shoes.
There was relief to know
we were no longer the only ones for whom
he'd weep, though this, too, was our trouble, our wound.

FIRST ESTRANGEMENT

I do not remember back then
when I was trying to leave one world
for the next, my girl-mother on the table,
all her darkness torn
for our two-headedness,

when around our violence floated
the universe, & we,
the naked astronauts
at our ends, at our beginnings,

years away from that staggering
out of one depth into another,
I remember her when I crack, again,
open the (already) starlight of the pomegranate,
when I bow my ear down toward it like a deer
without knowing why or from where
the hunger comes, faintly it screams

the memory of stars,
of estrangement, the lungs
pumping with air

how I take, & take
what I cannot give back

MOON FOR AISHA

—for Kamilah Aisha Moon, with a line after Cornelius Eady's "Gratitude"

Dear Aisha,
I mean to be writing you
a birthday letter, though it's not
September, the winter already
nearing, the bareness
of trees, their weightlessness,
their gestures—
grace or grief. The windows
of buildings all shining early, lit with light,
& I am only ten & riding
all of my horses home,
still sisterless, wanting sisters.

You do not know me yet.
In fact, we are years away
from that life. But I am thankful
for some inexplicable thing,
let's call it "freedom," or "night," the terror
& glee of being outside late, after dark,
my mother's voice shouting
for me beneath stars
which, I learned in school,
are suddenly not so different
from the small salt of fathers, & gratitude
for that, & for the red house of
your mother's blood,
& then, you, all nearly grown,
all long-legged laughter,
already knowing all the songs
& all the dances,
not *my* friend, yet,
but, somehow—Out There.

In one version of our lives,
it is November.
Through a window I see
one of our elders is
a black eye of a woman, is
a thinker, & magnificent. At a desk,
she builds her house with her hands,
with paper, wood & clay, the years of light
& the years of dark. She sees oblivion
& turns, crowns her head,
instead, with flowers,
the upper & the lower worlds.
Lightning streaks the black mind
of her hair, she leaves
it there, then cleans the house
with laughter, dances broadly
in each room, a pirouette,
a wop. Out of doors, she dares to wear
the house key from a silver hoop recalling
the moon, the gleaming syllable: of
a planet dark with fires & time.
She is glorious, isn't she?
It is always her birthday.
She has always lived
to tell a part
of the story of the world,
what happened here.

If not a moon, what can
we bring this woman who
walks ahead? For whom
you were named,
& whose name has been
added to by you
whose language crowns
the dark field of what has
been hushed, of what is
beautiful & black, & blue.

COOLEY HIGH, FIFTH ESTRANGEMENT
1991

I guess it's a funny thing, really,
    how I can't hear Boyz II Men,
even the 90s bedroom countdown
    & the color blue of Michael McCrary's
"Injection, fellas" without wanting
    to cry. A real cry. Look! I've slipped into
the surprise & trapdoor
    of my own heartache
just like that. The *Cooleyhighharmony*
    on repeat in the tape deck
as my mom & I drove up
    to boarding school, my first year. 1991.
& though I've tried, I can't stop being touched
    by the borrowed car, my mother's hands,
the steering wheel a kind of clock
    we moved with toward the finish line. We rode,
a slow unfurling of ourselves across
    a hundred twenty miles, despite history,
despite warnings of colored kids
    washed by books, or kerosene & lye
in the white yards of schools
    far from their fathers
& the stars. And still, hundreds of us
    tumbling out of our houses
to be half-raised. The ghosts of children
    from the Perris Indian School
did come down from the hills, all the way
    from Riverside, to watch the odd quiet
of our take-leavings. Their hairs thick
    with cactus & grave dirt. The prickly pears
of their mouths warning, *Some parts of you will*
    die there. I can still see it all
so clearly now. The school gate is—a carving knife.
    This is the future Mom chooses for me

& she drives me to my dormitory, room
     different from the one I woke in
beside my cousin & small sister, brother
     sleeping in the trundle. I have been thrown
into new orbit. This is
     an old story. Distance
in the name of opportunity.
     The complicated sacrifice,
& so on.
     But I could have stayed home
for so long. With my people.
     Helped around the house. Gotten a job.
In Chicago, my mother's hometown,
     the death toll climbs like a serpent up the red graph.
We are 2000 miles away, but the deaths of black
     kids everywhere are at her neck. So this is what
she chooses for me. I am not
     gifted, no more than Angel or Sargeant or LeNara
or most anybody, really,
     but know how to read & to obey the rules
of tests, & the academic officer
     says "hope" & "promise"
to my mother whose
     own mother would not choose my mother who
turns her back, & suddenly the car (with her hands)
     is leaving. I think, Who will be
my parent now? as the orange trees
     dot the coming darkness
with their small fires, & not far
     the sadness of oaks & dry brush. Still,
the car (with her hands) leaving.
     Please stay with me as I
replay the last touch. My face
     buried in her hair & neck. How
I am quiet, & let her say
     "This is the best thing"
though I disbelieve it, even now.

She was my mother, after all,
& president of nothing.

THE BEAUTY OF THE WORLD,
TENTH ESTRANGEMENT

It was Virgil's Aeneas who I loved,
whose devotion moved me
when he fled Troy holding his son's hand
& carrying his father. On the train
from Brindisi to Rome, they were the three
I thought of as the cars moved us through
our wherelessness, I who thought
I'd mastered this, I who only left & left,
& knew that I would not, in this world,
be Aeneas, & mourned my lack
of presence & character, & love,
that I had only ever carried my own head,
& into the other country, I who defended
the beauties of darkness (my worlds!)
in the grey, official halls of School
while my faces flashed with sorrow & rage,
I who started clear then, shamed,
learned to see home with an other-eye,
I who thought I could not love
both Virgil & Lumumba,
who secretly walked
with my flowers for them.

But it was grief I carried all along.
& it was love for my fathers,
in the country of Not-Love,
which caused me grief, & grief I carried
instead of love. Outside, the sunflower fields
—ploughed & harrowed—
said something to me about forgiveness.

Flower, forgive me.
Forgive me for the grief I held
instead of what I might have held.

Dark with rain, giving me back
the beauty of the world,
those fields made me weep.

SECOND ESTRANGEMENT

Please raise your hand,
whomever else of you
has been a child,
lost, in a market
or a mall, without
knowing it at first, following
a stranger, accidentally
thinking he is yours,
your family or parent, even
grabbing for his hands,
even calling the word
you said then for "Father,"
only to see the face
look strangely down, utterly
foreign, utterly not the one
who loves you, you
who are a bird suddenly
stunned by the glass partitions
of rooms.
                        How far
the world you knew, & tall,
& filled, finally, with strangers.

THIRD ESTRANGEMENT
in memory of Renisha McBride

Please raise your hand,
whomever else of you
has been a child,
lost,
      without
knowing it at first, following
a stranger, accidentally
thinking he is yours,
your family or   even
grabbing for his hands,
even calling the word
you said then for "Father,"
only to see the face
look strangely down, utterly
foreign, utterly not the one
who loves you, you
                  suddenly
stunned by the glass partitions

                  How far
the world you knew, & tall,
& filled, finally, with   angers.

THE BLACK MARIA

I.

after Neil deGrasse Tyson, black astrophysicist & director of the Hayden Planetarium, born in 1958, New York City. In his youth, deGrasse Tyson was confronted by police on more than one occasion when he was on his way to study stars.

"I've known that I've wanted to do astrophysics since I was nine years old, a first visit to the Hayden Planetarium... So I got to see how the world around me reacted to my expression of these ambitions. & all I can say is, the fact that I wanted to be a scientist, an astrophysicist, was, hands down, the path of most resistance... Anytime I expressed this interest teachers would say, Don't you want to be an athlete? Or, Don't you wanna... I wanted to become something that was outside of the paradigms of expectation of the people in power.

And I look behind me and say, Well, where are the others who might have been this? And they're not there. And I wonder, What is the [thing] along the tracks that I happened to survive and others did not? Simply because of the forces that prevented it. At every turn. At every turn."

—NdT, The Center for Inquiry, 2007

Body of space. Body of dark.
Body of light.

The Skyview apartments
      circa 1973, a boy is
kneeling on the rooftop, a boy who
      (it is important
to mention here his skin
      is brown) prepares his telescope,
the weights & rods,
      to better see the moon. His neighbor
(it is important to mention here
      that she is white) calls the police
because she suspects the brown boy
      of something, she does not know

what at first, then turns,
          with her looking,
his telescope into a gun,
          his duffel into a bag of objects
thieved from the neighbors' houses
          (maybe even hers) & the police
(it is important to mention
          that statistically they
are also white) arrive to find
          the boy who has been turned, by now,
into "the suspect," on the roof
          with a long, black lens, which is,
in the neighbor's mind, a weapon &
          depending on who you are, reading this,
you know that the boy is in grave danger,
          & you might have known
somewhere quiet in your gut,
          you might have worried for him
in the white space between lines 5 & 6,
          or maybe even earlier, & you might be holding
your breath for him right now
          because you know this story,
it's a true story, though,
          miraculously, in this version
of the story, anyway,
          the boy on the roof of the Skyview lives
to tell the police that he is studying
          the night & moon & lives
long enough to offer them (the cops) a view
          through his telescope's long, black eye, which,
if I am spelling it out anyway,
          is the instrument he borrowed
& the beautiful "trouble" he went through
          lugging it up to the roof
to better see the leopard body of
          space speckled with stars & the moon far off,
much farther than (since I am spelling *The Thing*

out) the distance between
the white neighbor who cannot see the boy
who is her neighbor, who,
in fact, is much nearer
to her than to the moon, the boy who
wants to understand the large
& gloriously un-human mysteries of
the galaxy, the boy who, despite "America,"
has not been killed by the murderous jury of
his neighbor's imagination & wound. This poem
wants only the moon in its hair & the boy on the roof.
This boy on the roof of this poem
with a moon in his heart. Inside my own body
as I write this poem my body
is making a boy even as the radio
calls out the Missouri coroner's news,
the Ohio coroner's news.
2015. My boy will nod
for his milk & close his mouth around
the black eye of my nipple.
We will survive. How did it happen?
The boy. The cops. My body in this poem.
My milk pulling down into droplets of light
as the baby drinks & drinks them down
into the body that is his own, see it,
splayed & sighing as a star in my arms.
Maybe he will be the boy who studies stars.
Maybe he will be (say it)
the boy on the coroner's table
splayed & spangled
by an officer's lead as if he, too, weren't made
of a trillion glorious cells & sentences. Trying to last.

Leadless, remember? The body's beginning,
splendored with breaths, turned,
by time, into, at least, this song.

This moment-made & the mackerel-"soul"
caught flashing inside the brief moment of the body's net,
then, whoosh, back into the sea of space.

The poem dreams of bodies always leadless, bearing
only things ordinary
as water & light.

II.
I, too, am built out of a question about the sky,
a body bearing things ordinary as light,
& when I realized this I was on my back, my legs
in the stirrups & the lights of the technician's office
were dimmed as she slid the wand up
inside me after, like a room, the baby emptied
me, & "space" is what I thought
as the technician clicked her machine for a close-up
here & there & there, which was really all me &
the seeming limitlessness of my body's dark,
how did I spend so many years dismarveling the body
its powers & beauties, thinking the world a place
I did not belong to, thinking myself alien,
though, of course, it was always ever my only home,
& in that room my heart, then, had a brazen dream & drew,
with its brown fingers, its own curtains back
so that I could see the courtyard inside it
where the peacocks swept the dirt
with the dark of their closed tails
within which the green burned secretly
like a fever & I saw my six words & their ghosts
& the mothers nodding
from beneath the pepper tree & a well
at the center of the yard of my heart,
& I held the dead-given pail
so lowered it down into my chest,
then up, &, like that, was taught
by the elders
to lift sorrow out
from my sorrow.

III.
This poem
wants only the moon in its hair & the boy on the roof.
This boy on the roof of this poem
with a moon in his heart.

Splayed & sighing as a star in my arms.
Maybe he will be the boy who studies stars.

IV.
What verbs will I use
to describe the living of my beloveds?

Beloveds, if I love,
what language will I
love you in   If I see
what language will I use to see

& if I love & if I see
you   Then strike lines across
the terrorful verbs, write:

"love," "study," "make," "disturb."

V.
Somewhere I got the idea
to keep them separate:
this story from that one,
these stars from those,
the history of this sea from
the history of that sea.
Separating the body into territories
of easy sense while overhead,
the sky marked by light
is read in the constellations of
someone else's myth.

But the angles I chart
abide by different sight
& hover up not
as bears or sisters but
a route dense with fires,
dark time adorned by
the messages of mirrors
saying: you are made with every where.

VI.
D. is in
the hospital room
& the white nurse, when she says
"He is lucky," I know, means
not lucky to be "alive"
but lucky to be in "America"
as if he were not always
trying to get home,
as if there were not
trees & rivers there.
She speaks loudly.
Tries to remember
how to *connect*.
Tries to rush through.
Her English is an Empire
and imagines only itself.

We tell her in our way:
Slow down,
not your language, but
your eye.
See him.

> *Body of sight. Body of*
> *breaths. Body of trying.*

How he carries his weight, even now,
with great effort, so as not to burden
you.

But her job, this country
does not require this of her
so she is gone already,
already out of sight, & doors.

VII.

Body of sight. Body of
breaths. Body of trying.

Beloved, to
day you eat,
today you bathe, today
you laugh

Today you walk,
today you read,
today you paint, my love,

Today you study stars,
today you write,
today you climb the stairs,

Today you run,
today you see,
today you talk,

You cut the basil
You sweep the floor

& as you chore, touch
the ankles & hairs of your befores
who look up from their work
in the field or at the chisel
to tell you in their ways: You Live!

VIII.
  How did it happen?
  The boy. The cops. My body in this poem.

The body, bearing something ordinary as light   Opens

as in a room somewhere the friend opens in poppy, in flame, burns &
bears the child—out.

When I did it was the hours & hours of breaking. The bucking of
it all, the push & head

not moving, not an inch until,
when he flew from me, it was the night who came

flying through me with all its hair,
the immense terror of his face & noise.

I heard the stranger & my brain, without looking, vowed
a love him vow. His struggling, merely, to be

split me down, with the axe, to two. How true,
the thinness of our hovering between the realms of Here, Not Here.

The fight, first, to open, then to breathe,
& then to close. Each of us entering the world

& entering the world like this.
Soft. Unlikely.   Then—

the idiosyncratic minds & verbs.
    Beloveds, making your ways

to & away from us, always, across the centuries,
inside the vastness of the galaxy, how improbable it is that this iteration

of you or you or me might come to be at all—Body of fear,
Body of laughing—& even last a second. This fact should make us fall all

to our knees with awe,
the beauty of it against these odds,

the stacks & stacks of near misses
& slimmest chances that birthed one ancestor into the next & next.

Profound, unspeakable cruelty who counters this, who does not see.

& so to tenderness I add my action.

FOURTH ESTRANGEMENT, WITH A PETITION FOR THE REUNION OF JONATHAN & GEORGE JACKSON

—passing the island of San Michele, Venice

Though we rushed, in our way, through
    the tangle of streets,
        the green world & the red world,
& though, from the docks,
    there stood San Michele not so far off,
        we were late, it was not our time.

We boarded anyway, knowing
    the boat would take us
        only to Murano & then back,
to Cannaregio, again, 10 minutes
    each way, if that, but we wanted
        to pass, to see

the walls' precision,
    the beauty of brick aged & worn
        by water, by air,
an island of coffins risen, & rectangles risen
    from the sea, improbably,
        & all I could think was the word "Brodsky"

who visited Venice 17 Decembers, who said
    "Leaving all of the world, all its blue…,"
        who was buried there
among the officers & the cypress trees,
    the island's histories of
        the quiet of monks

& the prisoners' pens, then
    the gondolas laden with flowers, then
        the coming of dusk,
then the lights & fog,

the new century's traffic
of boats & the apple eye of the moon

nearly full as we passed San Michele
thinking, We cannot stop there now
but will touch the other shore,
desolate with its stacked chairs
& signs for no one at this hour, we will
touch & then turn back

toward Cannaregio,
home of history's first ghetto,
a Jewish ghetto,
& the one wooden ladder we saw on our return,
which makes me think, only now, of Jacob
& his dream, this ladder which did, that evening,

seem to aim toward a height that was not heaven
but suggested heaven, propped as it was
against the high wall, the darkness
absorbing its final gesture. If we
had believed, we would have looked
for the dark faces of angels, climbing the ladder

& falling, carrying with them the messages
of exile, but, instead, there was just
the beauty of
the ladder against a wall, which is
a different beauty than the beauty of
a ladder on its side, or in a tree,

for our parents had been
locked out before.
In Cannaregio,
the gates & guards,
the three brothers
locked in stone,

    & the Jews inside the ghetto walls
        repeating their sentences of worth
                to themselves, to god, under
their breaths, over their meals,
        into their clothes as they mended
                & endured the uncertain hours

behind the gate where, year after year at Passover,
        the din of families & light,
                lamentations, the story
of slavery in Egypt, the plagues,
        first of blood, then frogs, until
                the tenth plague, the angel

of death killing the firstborn
        of each human, of even the
                donkey, of even the cattle,
passing over only the doors marked
        with the secret blood of lambs,
                the doors of the chosen

until the Pharaoh's final relent
        & the Exodus of the Israelites,
                forging the covenant of the Jews
with God. That was faith & metaphor.
        The Book of Exodus.
                Yet it would come to serve them through

the other sentences, & years. Look at what a story can do.
        Astonishing what a story can do.
                Who would we who were enslaved be now
had that been the story we told
        ourselves of ourselves? A chosenness by God.
                No afterlife. No poverty now & gold in heaven. No balm.

What changes? Does not change?
        What if the enslavement & The Severances

were seen as persecution of our own black godliness?
Our holiness or specialness? Except, instead, I believe
 the terror & the beauty that the water teaches:
  no one is special, no one is special,

so let us keep learning as our mothers do,
 loving women, loving men,
  washing the feet of the beloved
at birth, at death, saying hello,
 & cultivating questions
  beside our joy.

I am caring now about Jonathan,
 not David's, son of Jacob,
  Jonathan,
but son of Lester & Georgia,
 youngest Brother of George. Jonathan who saw his George
  stolen, who saw his genius locked away,[1]

Jonathan Jackson who was seventeen &,
 for a moment, free,[2] who tried to make
  his body a Ladder Out
of loyalty, out of love.
 Who is now not
  dreaming under stars, but gone

from all his life & all his beauty,
 & George, killed in bright sun
  by the prison guard's morbid aim,
George who wrote his letters
 with his back to the wall,
  in ugly & artificial light,

full of sorrow & of rage
 & always only ever full of love

---

[1] from "George Moses Horton, Myself" by George Moses Horton
[2] from *Soledad Brother: The Prison Letters of George Jackson*

in San Quentin, circled
by the San Francisco Bay, & not far,
   beneath time, then, now,
         the Pacific turning & turning

its infinitely black pages, black
   with the names,
         & though it truly wounds us to believe
in death, gone Jonathan, gone
   George, the countless falling out of
         memory's frame into the sea's roiling behavior,

I know that death is also real
   & with my bit of life petition
         for the reunion of Jonathan & George,
& while I'm at it, Virgil Lamar & James Jr. Ware,
   because *there are stars, but none of you, to spare,*[3]
         & Margaret Garner & her child, & Abraham

& Sahalu, & they to the grass & a view of the moon,
   the baobab & the oak & the acacia,
         & they to the taste of clean water from
the river & dirt the color of their mothers' hands
   to eat from. Time fools me into thinking
         they have not lasted, but let me tie

the breath that I borrow to
   the breath that you borrow, let
         them meet through the green
that is you & that is me,
   & knowing what we know now
         of history & of love,

let us name every air between strangers "Reunion."

---

[3] from "Sunflower Sonnet Number Two" by June Jordan

NOTES

elelegy

"elelelele," if repeated enough, conjures the ululatory sounds people make in many places (Eritrea, a central location of the project, and my father's homeland, among them). *elelegy* means to place itself in both the English elegiac tradition and the ulalatory traditions of grieving and joy in cultures of North and East Africa.

Section II of *"prayer & letter to the dead"* ends with a line inspired by Marianne Moore's "men lower nets, unconscious of the fact that they are desecrating / a grave" (from "A Grave).

Section VI of *"prayer & letter to the dead"* mentions, for the first time, Israel alongside Italy and the United States. It is estimated that over 30,000 Eritreans are currently in Israel seeking political asylum though in recent years Human Rights Watch estimates the rejection of 99.9% of Eritrean (and Sudanese) political asylum claims. In the last few years, human rights organizations have criticized the Israeli government's severe and harsh treatment of African refugees.

"hands for pleasure, hands for mending" (p. 29) is inspired by Patrick Rosal's "Dream of the Girl with Eight Limbs."

"To be near sea is to gleam" (p. 42) includes a line inspired by Gwendolyn Brooks' "Those people. / Visiting the world as I visit the world" (from "The Near-Johannesburg Boy").

"luam, new york" (p.49) holds Shane McCrae's poem that begins "Dear Once-Incarnate-   Silence dear" (from *Mule*) deep inside its ear.

Lastly, I am indebted to Ilya Kaminsky whose use of brackets in *Dancing in Odessa* helped me to find a form for my notes to exist in the body of the cycle.

"Third Estrangement, in Memory of Jonathan Ferrell": 24-year-old Jonathan Ferrell was killed by 29-year-old Randall Kerrick, a white police officer, on September 14, 2013, while seeking help after a car accident. In August of 2015, North Carolina judge Robert C. Ervin declared a mistrial after the jury reached a deadlock (eight jurors on one side and four on the other). Ferrell was (*is*) the son of Georgia Ferrell. He was engaged to Caché Heidel, and was a former football player.

"Moon for Aisha": The lines "She has always lived / to tell a part / of the story of the world" are inspired by the following lines from Cornelius Eady's poem "Gratitude": "I have survived / long enough / to tell a bit / Of an old story."

"Cooley High, Fifth Estrangement": The Perris Indian School, now known as The Sherman Indian School, was established in 1892 under the direction of Mr. M. S. Savage. It was the first off-reservation Indian Boarding School in California. Students ranged in age from 5 years old to their early 20s. These boarding schools were part of a violent assimilation initiative under the U.S. government and many of these children were essentially kidnapped or taken from their families against their and their family's will. Because many children were not allowed to return home for several years, there was a cemetery on the school grounds for the children who died at school.

"Third Estrangement": Renisha McBride was killed by a white homeowner on November 2, 2013, after knocking on the door and windows of his house.

"Fourth Estrangement, with a Petition for the Reunion of Jonathan & George Jackson": San Michele is an island in Venice, Italy, and it has served as the city's official cemetery since the 1800s. The island holds Chiesa di San Michele in Isola, one of the early Renaissance churches of Venice. The island has also housed a monastery, and, for a time, served as a prison.

Cannaregio is one of the six historic districts of Venice and Isola di San Michele can be seen from its banks. For nearly 300 years, Jewish residents were forced to live in the Venetian Ghetto in this district. The ghetto was enclosed by guarded gates and its residents weren't allowed to leave from dusk to dawn.

George Jackson (September 23, 1941–August 21, 1971) was an activist, Black Panther Party member, and writer. Note from introduction to *Soledad Brother: The Prison Letters of George Jackson*:

> In 1960, at the age of eighteen, George Jackson was accused of stealing $70 from a gas station in Los Angeles. Though there was evidence of his innocence, his court-appointed lawyer maintained that because Jackson had a record (two previous instances of petty crime), he should plead guilty in exchange for a light sentence in the county jail. He did, and received an indeterminate sentence of one year to life. Jackson spent the next ten years in Soledad Prison, seven and a half of them in solitary confinement. [In prison he became] the leading theoretician of the prison movement and a brilliant writer. *Soledad Brother*, which contains the letters that he wrote from 1964 to 1970, is his testament.

George Jackson was killed by a prison guard in 1971.

Jonathan Jackson (June 23, 1953–August 7, 1970) was the brother of George Jackson and youngest child of Georgia Bea and Lester Jackson. Jonathan Jackson is most known for momentarily taking a judge and three jurors hostage in his attempt to negotiate the freedom of the Soledad Brothers (including his brother George). At the age of 17 Jonathan Jackson was killed in this attempt. His son, Jonathan Jackson, Jr., was born 8 and ½ months later and would go on to become a writer and wrote the foreword to his uncle George's *Soledad Brother* prison letters. From that foreword:

> I was born eight and a half months after my father, Jonathan Jackson, was shot down on Aug. 7, 1970, at the Marin County Courthouse, when he tried to gain the release of the Soledad Brothers by taking hostages. Before and especially after that day, Uncle George kept in constant contact with my mother by writing from his cell in San Quentin. (The Department of Corrections wouldn't put her on the visitors' list.) During George's numerous trial appearances for the Soledad Brothers case, Mom would lift me above the crowd so he could see me. Consistently, we would receive a letter a few days

later. For a single mother with son, alone and in the middle of both controversy and not a little unwarranted trouble with the authorities, those messages of strength were no doubt instrumental in helping her carry on. No matter how oppressive his situation became, George always had time to lend his spirit to the people he cared for.

ACKNOWLEDGMENTS

My gratitude to the editors of the following publications in which these poems, sometimes in earlier versions, first appeared:

Academy of American Poets Poem-a-Day project: "The Woodlice";
Black Renaissance Noire: "Third Estrangement, in Memory of Jonathan Ferrell," "The Beauty of the World, Tenth Estrangement";
Granta: "Cooley High, Fifth Estrangement";
Harvard Review: Section I of "The Black Maria";
Muzzle: "*to the sea near lampedusa*";
PEN Poetry Series: "Odysseus, his lungs full," "Claim, I, to be the poet, making talk";
The Prairie Schooner: "*prayer & letter to the dead,*" "*luam to the dead,*" "*luam mending clothes,*" "*luam & the flies*";
The Wide Shore: "First Estrangement," "*luam, monterchi, italy.*"

*

for the world must be loved this much —nâzim hikmet
I have struggled with this particular project, so steeped in violence, mourning, and grief. How do I work inside of such histories of violence without further brutalizing the black body in the work? How do I, especially here, make critical space for joy and tenderness in the remembering, so that my own imagination (gesture by gesture, line by line) isn't rendered by the values of white supremacy or violence as I resist it? And how do I express, with tenderness, who and what this work/I love(s)? It is my hope that while these poems mourn the dead and the bleak circumstances of our present, violent day, they are also a tribute to black joy, black art, black making, black life. There are many who walk beside and ahead, and who show, in their lives and work, how I might do this better, among them: Tebereh Tesfahunegn, June Jordan, Lucille Clifton, Audre Lorde, James Baldwin, Asres Tessema, Reesom Haile, Nikky Finney, Elizabeth Alexander, Cornelius Eady, Toi Derricotte, the Turf Feinz, Araia Ephrem, Chris Abani, Kwame Dawes, Huriy Ghirmai, Martín Espada, M. Estefanos. And: I am deeply grateful to the following people who challenge and nourish the effort behind my seeing: Lisa Ascalon, Uzma Aslam Kahn, Elana Bell, Haile Berhe, Amina

Blacksher, Maryam Blacksher, Cheryl Boyce Taylor, Rosalba Campra, Ama Codjoe, Nandi Comer, Erica Doyle, Kathy Engle, Shira Erlichman, Vaughan Fielder, David Flores, Tanya Gallo, Roberto Garcia, Daphne and Saultas Gibbs, Dagoberto Gilb, Deb Gorlin, Rachel Eliza Griffiths, Laurie Ann Guerrero, Parneshia Jones, Steffie Kinglake, N.S. Köenings, Michele Kotler, Robin Coste Lewis, Kara Lynch, Anne Marie Macari, Heather Madden, Paola Marcus Carranza, Shane McCrae, Jane Mead, Anna Molitor, Erin Molitor, Yesenia Montilla, Mihaela Moscaliuc, Alison Meyers, Sean Nevin, Alicia Ostriker, Stephanos Papadopoulous, Cergio Prudencio, Carla Repice, Will Ryan, the Salandys, Erynn Sampson, Ruth Irupé Sanabria, John Sands, Matthew Shenoda, Ellie Siegel, Gerald Stern, Sandy Taylor, Samantha Thornhill, Chris Tinson, Mark Underwood, Rich Villar, Jean Valentine, Judith Vollmer, Michael Waters, Ellen Watson, Renée Watson, Simone White, Marina Wilson, Maaria Wirkkala. Thank you to: Peter Conners, Melissa Hall, Jenna Fisher, Sandy Knight, Richard Foerster, and BOA Editions, for your kindness and care; Kamilah Aisha Moon and Laure-Anne Bosselaar, for leading me here; my "students," too many to name, for your generosity and for your example; Ellen Hagan, for your gold heart and friendship, for your work and questions for this manuscript; Patrick Rosal and Ross Gay, my first readers, dear eyes, my dear friends; Marcelitte Failla, Kjerstin Rossi, Magnus Rosengarten, for your collaboration on The Experiment. To my parents, my siblings, and cousins: what life you've watered my trying with. Rassan Salandy, for what is tender, joyful, and courageous, for your commitment to asking and saying what is difficult—out of love.

For your support and encouragement, thank you: Acentos (always), Cave Canem, CantoMundo, Civitella Ranieri, PSA, the Whiting Foundation, the Vermont Studio Center, louderARTS. Camille Dungy, Rigoberto González, Angel Nafis, Lynne Procope: you have adorned the doors with gold and flowers and, in your ways, made so much room for the many to walk through. Thank you.

Finally, I bow to those who walk ahead: H. Z. H. K. L. G. And to those (Alem!) who walk behind, teaching us about joy and effort especially in the midst of grief: I will work to deserve you. Thank you.

To the many others who, for the sake of discretion, I will not mention here: ye'anyelay. The poems are inadequate, but I mean for them to serve as my small and ongoing bouquet of flowersmemorysong, all the same. It is my hope that these poems honor you in some way. The opinions and mistakes are my own.

ABOUT THE AUTHOR

Aracelis Girmay grew up in California where, companioned by the idea of a large and mighty Pacific, her *awe* of the sea was born. Girmay is the author of the poetry collections *Teeth* (Curbstone Press) and *Kingdom Animalia* (BOA), for which she was awarded the GLCA New Writers Award and was a finalist for the National Book Critics Circle Award respectively. *Kingdom Animalia* was also a finalist for the Hurston/Wright Legacy Award. She also wrote/collaged the picture book *changing, changing* (George Braziller). Her poems have appeared in *Granta*, *The Prairie Schooner*, *The Wide Shore*, and *Indiana Review*, among other places. Her honors include a Whiting Writers Award and fellowships from Cave Canem, Civitella Ranieri, and the NEA. She teaches in Hampshire College's School for Interdisciplinary Arts and Drew University's low-residency MFA program in poetry.

BOA EDITIONS, LTD.
AMERICAN POETS CONTINUUM SERIES

COLOPHON

BOA Editions, Ltd., a not-for-profit publisher of poetry and other literary works, fosters readership and appreciation of contemporary literature. By identifying, cultivating, and publishing both new and established poets and selecting authors of unique literary talent, BOA brings high-quality literature to the public. Support for this effort comes from the sale of its publications, grant funding, and private donations.

The publication of this book is made possible, in part, by the special support of the following individuals:

Anonymous x 3
Nin Andrews
Angela Bonazinga & Catherine Lewis
Nickole Brown & Jessica Jacobs
Bernadette Catalana
Christopher & DeAnna Cebula
Gwen & Gary Conners
Anne C. Coon & Craig J. Zicari
Gouvernet Arts Fund
Michael Hall, *in memory of Lorna Hall*
Grant Holcomb
Christopher Kennedy & Mi Ditmar
X. J. & Dorothy M. Kennedy
Keetje Kuipers & Sarah Fritsch, *in memory of JoAnn Wood Graham*
Jack & Gail Langerak
Daniel M. Meyers, *in honor of James Shepard Skiff*
Boo Poulin
Deborah Ronnen & Sherman Levey
Steven O. Russell & Phyllis Rifkin-Russell
Sue S. Stewart, *in memory of Stephen L. Raymond*
Lynda & George Waldrep
Michael Waters & Mihaela Moscaliuc
Michael & Patricia Wilder

❀